I0165232

Old Jack's Ghost Stories from Ireland

I Talk You Talk Press

Copyright © 2018 I Talk You Talk Press

ISBN: 978-4-907056-64-3

www.italkyoutalk.com

info@italkyoutalk.com

All rights reserved. No part of this publication may be resold, reproduced, stored in retrieval system, copied in any form or by any means, electronic, mechanical, photocopying, recording or otherwise transmitted without the prior written permission from the publisher. You must not circulate this publication in any format, online or otherwise.

This book contains ghost stories found in sources in the public domain. We have rewritten the stories to ensure they fit into the appropriate level. All source materials (websites, books) consulted in the writing of these stories have been referenced and appear at the rear of this publication. We make no claims regarding the truth of the ghost stories in this book and accept no responsibility for any information from referenced third party sources.

Although the author and publisher have made every effort to ensure that the contents of this book were correct at press time, the author and publisher do not assume and hereby disclaim any liability to any party for any loss, damage, or disruption caused by errors or omissions, whether such errors or omissions result from negligence, accident, or any other cause.

Image copyright: © deviantART - Fotolia.com #36718905 Standard License

CONTENTS

ACKNOWLEDGMENTS

With sincere thanks to Colin Dixon who collected and recorded the stories contained in this volume. Without his contribution this book would not have been possible.

MESSAGE FROM OLD JACK

Hello my friends! Welcome to my fourth book of ghost stories. In this book, we travel to Ireland, to hear some stories and legends. We visit the Republic of Ireland, and we also cross the border and travel to Northern Ireland.

If you visited Ireland, you would understand why it is called the Emerald Isle. It is a beautiful country, with lots of greenery. It also has a long history. In some of the history there are religious and political divisions, but this book is not about those divisions. This book is about the division between life and death...between the world of the living, and the world of the dead...

I was very lucky when I visited Ireland. My friend, Peter Connor, from County Meath, took me on a tour of the country, and he told me many stories.

So, come and join Peter and me, as we travel around this beautiful scenic island, and discover its dark secrets...

1. CROMWELL'S FRIEND

Place: Malahide Castle, County Dublin

I met my friend, Peter Connor, in a pub in Dublin last winter. We hadn't seen each other for a long time. We enjoyed a few glasses of smooth Irish whiskey while we talked about our lives. As the sky outside started to darken, and evening came, Peter said to me, "Let me tell you about Malahide Castle. We are going there tomorrow. Sometimes strange things happen there."

I put my glass of whiskey down on the table, took my notebook and pen out of my bag, and listened to Peter. This is what he told me:

Malahide Castle was built in the 12th century, by Henry II (the second) of England. He built it for his friend, Sir Richard Talbot. The Talbot family owned the castle until 1979. Now, it is owned by the government, and people can visit it. It's a very popular tourist spot near Dublin. Many old castles have a ghost, but Malahide Castle doesn't just have one ghost. It has many ghosts. Some people say it has three, other people say it has even more. One of the ghosts is the "white lady". Some people have seen her walking around the great hall. Another ghost is a court jester called Puck. Sometimes, he appears in tourists' photographs!

But these ghosts are not the most frightening ghosts in the castle. No, the most frightening ghost is called Miles Corbet.

Let's go back to the 17th century, to the English Civil War. This war was between King Charles I (the first) and the government. A chief member of the government was Oliver Cromwell. He hated the King. He fought many battles against the army of King Charles.

Miles Corbet was a very good friend and supporter of Oliver Cromwell.

King Charles I was defeated in the war, and he was arrested. Fifty-nine of Cromwell's friends and supporters signed a document. The document said, ---*The King must die.*---

One of the fifty-nine men who signed the document was Cromwell's friend, Miles Corbet. Soon after, King Charles I was killed.

Cromwell became the leader of the government. He wanted to thank Corbet for his support, so he gave Malahide Castle to Corbet. The Talbot family lost their home. This was in 1649.

Corbet was not a nice man. He was very strict, and he didn't like the Roman Catholics in Ireland. He sent soldiers to make trouble at the local church, and he tried to ban the Roman Catholic religion. The local people hated him.

A few years later, Cromwell died. The government needed a new leader. They couldn't find anyone. So they asked the son of Charles I, who was also called Charles, to become king.

Charles said 'yes'. At that time, he was living in mainland Europe. He returned to England, and became King Charles II (the second). But he was still angry about his father's death. He said, 'All the fifty-nine men who signed the document saying my father must die, must be arrested and killed!'

Corbet heard this and panicked. He ran away and went overseas. The Talbot family returned to their castle. In 1662, Corbet was found. He was arrested, and taken back to England. He was hanged from a rope until he was nearly dead. Then, the soldiers cut him down from the rope, broke his bones, and cut off his arms and legs with a sword, while he was still alive. It was a terrible way to die.

When Peter finished telling me the story, he said, "We will go to the castle tomorrow morning. I have booked a guided tour for us."

The next day, Peter and I went to Malahide Castle. It was a cold, cloudy day, and the sky was grey. There were only a few other tourists. After the tour, we walked around the gardens outside.

"Well, we didn't see any ghosts. What does the ghost of Miles Corbet look like?" I asked Peter.

"Well," said Peter. "People say he wears a soldier's uniform. It is the uniform of Cromwell's soldiers."

"Have many tourists seen him?" I asked.

"Oh yes. Some visitors have been walking around the castle, enjoying their visit. Then, at the end of a hall, or at the top of the stairs, they see a man, wearing a soldier's uniform. He looks very nervous. He looks like he can't relax. Then, when he sees the visitors, he starts to walk towards them. Of course, the visitors become frightened. Then, the man's face changes. When he sees that the visitors are looking at him, he becomes angry."

"What do the visitors do?"

"Some try to run away, but others are too frightened. They stand still, and watch the man coming towards them. Then, something strange happens. The man cannot walk very well. He looks like he is in pain. Suddenly, his arms and legs fall off, and his uniform becomes red. It is covered in blood. His body falls to the floor. Then, his body slowly disappears."

Suddenly I felt very cold.

"Is the ending always the same?" I asked Peter.

"Oh yes, it is. It has happened many times, and all the visitors who have seen him tell the same story."

I looked up at the castle. *I'm glad I didn't see that,* I thought.

2. COMING HOME

Place: Castle Leslie, Glaslough, County Monaghan

For our next story, we travel to the village of Glaslough, which is near the border with Northern Ireland. The place is Castle Leslie. Now, it is a luxury hotel, with beautiful rooms, a spa and restaurants. It has a lake and lots of parkland. Today, visitors have a relaxing time in this beautiful location. It is often called Europe's most romantic hotel, and is a popular place for weddings.

For this story, we go back to 1914. Norman Leslie, the son of the family, had gone away to France, to fight in the First World War. His family missed him very much, and they were worried about him.

One sunny day, when Norman was in France, a servant looked out of the window and saw a man. The man was standing on the terrace. She ran out to the terrace and said,

"Master Norman! Master Norman! Is that you? You've come back! This is a wonderful surprise! I'll tell everyone! They will be very happy."

The servant ran through the castle. She found the other servants.

"Quick! Everyone! Get Master Norman's room ready! Prepare some food! He has come back!"

"Really? He's come back? I don't believe it!" said one of the maids. The servant and the maid ran back to the terrace.

"Where is he?" asked the maid. She looked around, but she couldn't see him.

The servant looked around. "But...but...he was here. I promise you. I saw him. It was Master Norman. He was wearing his soldier's uniform."

The man had gone.

One night, a few weeks later, Lady Marjorie, a member of the Leslie family, was sleeping in her bed, when she suddenly woke up. A soft white light filled the room. She sat up, and saw Norman. He was standing near her bed, looking at some letters.

"Norman, what are you doing here?" asked Lady Marjorie.

Norman looked at her and smiled. Then, he disappeared.

Soon after, a message arrived from the government. Norman had been killed in France. At the time the servant saw him on the terrace, he had been fighting in a terrible battle in France. He was killed a week later.

In the battle, he had used a sword. His enemies had used machine guns. He was soon killed.

Later, his brother went to France to get Norman's sword. He brought it back to Castle Leslie. We can still see this sword today. It is hanging in the gallery.

Peter and I had afternoon tea in Castle Leslie. As we ate our scones and drank our tea, we talked about Norman.

"It's an interesting story," I said. "Norman's ghost appeared on the terrace before he died. I think that is unusual."

"Yes," said Peter. "I think so too. Maybe he wanted to say goodbye. Maybe he wanted to see his home one last time. It's very strange."

"So do people see Norman's ghost today?" I asked.

"Some people have seen him. His old bedroom is now a hotel room for guests. Some people have woken up in the middle of the night, and seen a white light. In the centre of the white light is a young man. He is looking for something. When they try and talk to him, he disappears," said Peter.

"Where did Lady Marjorie see Norman's ghost?"

"It was in the Red Room. The Red Room is a very popular room for visitors. They have heard the story about Norman, and they want to stay in it. Lady Marjorie used the room until she died in 1951."

Peter moved closer to me and said quietly, "Norman is not the only ghost in the family. Lady Marjorie, who saw the ghost of Norman in her room, had a son. Her son got married and moved to London. Later, Lady Marjorie became old, and she died. At the moment she died, her ghost appeared in her son's apartment in

London. It's very strange."

"Yes, it is very strange," I said. I finished my tea. I was ready for a whiskey.

3. KNOCK KNOCK

Place: Ballygally Castle, Ballygally, County Antrim

For our next story, we leave County Monaghan and travel across the border into Northern Ireland. We are going to Ballygally, a small village around forty kilometres from Belfast.

Our story is about Ballygally Castle Hotel. The castle was built in 1625 by James Shaw of Scotland. In the 1950s, a building was attached to the castle, and it became a hotel. Guests can stay in the hotel section, or the old castle section.

The hotel is in a beautiful location, near the sea. People come here to relax, and enjoy the wonderful scenery and fresh air.

As we were driving through Northern Ireland, Peter said to me, "Old Jack, I have a surprise for you. We are going to stay in Ballygally Castle Hotel tonight. I have reserved rooms for us, but we are not staying in the hotel section. We are staying in the original castle section."

"Oh, that's wonderful!" I said.

Peter smiled. "I hope you still think it's wonderful in the morning," he said.

I looked at him. "What do you mean?" I asked.

"Well, the hotel often has more ghosts than guests," said Peter.

"Pardon? More ghosts than guests? So there are many ghosts?"

Peter smiled. "Yes. And they come out at night, when the guests are sleeping."

After dinner that night, I went to my room. It was next to Peter's room. It was cold and windy outside, and the sea was rough and noisy. I stood at the window, listening to the dark sea. A few minutes later, Peter knocked on the door.

"Shall we walk around? I'll tell you a story," he said.

As we walked through the old hallways, Peter told me about Isobel Shaw.

Isobel Shaw was the wife of James Shaw. Isobel gave birth to a daughter. But James was very angry when the baby was born. He took Isobel up to a small corner room in the castle turret, overlooking the sea, and locked the door. He would not let her come out of the room. Some people say he was angry because Isobel didn't have a son. Other people say he was angry because Isobel had had a relationship with a sailor, and the child was not James's. The baby was the sailor's. We will never know. But we do know that Isobel's daughter was taken away from her, and she was locked in the corner room, with no food. She wanted to escape and see her daughter, so she jumped out of the small window to the ground below. She died.

Peter stopped outside a room.

"This is it," he said. The hotel workers call this the 'Ghost Room'. No guests can stay in this room. Only the ghost of Isobel Shaw is in this room."

"This room is above my room!" I said.

"Yes," said Peter. "And many people in your room, and my room, have had very strange experiences. At night, they wake up. Someone is knocking on the door. They open the door. But no one is there."

I suddenly felt cold. "Is it the ghost of Isobel Shaw? Does she knock on the door?" I asked.

"I don't know. Maybe. Some guests have heard children running and laughing in their rooms. They look for the children, but they cannot see them. They can only hear them."

"Who are the children?" I asked.

"I don't know. Maybe some of the ghosts are children. Perhaps one of the children is Isobel's daughter. Perhaps she is looking for her mother."

"That's sad," I said. "Has anyone ever seen Isobel?"

"Some guests have seen a woman in their rooms at night. When they sit up and try to look at the woman, she disappears."

We started to walk back down the stairs to our rooms. *Maybe two of the ghosts are those of Isobel and her daughter,* I thought. Maybe they will be walking around the castle, looking for each other, forever.

We stopped outside our rooms. "Good night, Peter," I said.

"Good night, Old Jack."

I walked into my room, switched the light on, and locked the door behind me.

I lay on my bed and listened to the rough sea outside. I looked at the clock. It was 10:30pm. *Time to go to sleep,* I thought. I got changed and got into bed. I switched my bedside lamp off. Then, it happened.

Knock knock.

I sat up. *What was that?* I thought.

Knock knock. There was someone knocking on my door! I switched the lamp on, got out of bed and very quietly walked to the door. I turned the door handle very slowly and opened the door. I could see the shadow of a person...

"Peter!" I shouted. "What are you doing? You frightened me! I thought you were the ghost of Isobel Shaw!"

"Sorry Old Jack. I didn't want to frighten you. I forgot to ask you a question."

"What is it?"

"What time are you getting up tomorrow?"

"Six am!"

"OK," said Peter. "Good night, Old Jack."

"Peter, don't knock on my door in the middle of the night!" I said.

"Of course not, Old Jack. I won't do it again. If you hear someone knocking on your door, it won't be me. Good night!"

Peter went back to his room. I got back into bed.

I think I will sleep with the light on tonight, I thought.

4. THE BETRAYAL

Place: Springhill House, Moneymore, County Londonderry/Derry

Before leaving Northern Ireland, Peter took me to County Londonderry, or County Derry as it is also known. Even in winter, the countryside was beautiful. We passed a wonderful lake, called Lough Neagh. This is the largest lake in Northern Ireland, and many people come to the lake to enjoy the scenery. It is a popular bird watching place. Peter told me that birdwatchers come from all over the world to see the winter birds on the lake. We drove away from the lake, and travelled through green fields and farmland. We soon arrived at Springhill House. It was a big, white building, with large grounds and a garden.

"This looks wonderful," I said. "Can we go inside?"

"It's not open in winter, but we can walk around the grounds," said Peter.

We got out of the car and walked towards the house.

"How old is this place?" I asked.

"Seventeenth century," said Peter. "It has a long history."

"Is there a ghost?" I asked.

Peter laughed. "Of course there is, Old Jack! That's why I brought you here!"

Then, he stopped laughing. "It's a very sad story. Are you sure you want to hear it?"

"Oh yes," I said.

"Well, from the seventeenth century to nineteen fifty-seven, the

Conyngham family owned this house. In nineteen fifty-seven, they gave it to the National Trust. Anyway, long ago, in eighteen fourteen, George Lenox-Conyngham lived here with his wife and children.

"George was in the British army, so he was often away from home. One night, he was on guard. When a soldier is on guard, he cannot easily leave his place. He must stay on duty until the next soldier comes. But George got some bad news. His children were very sick. He was very worried. He thought his children might die. He had to go home. He had to go back to Springhill House and see his children."

"But he couldn't. He was on guard, right?" I said.

"He couldn't. But he did. He was so worried. He left the place and started to go back. On the way back, he saw his officer - his boss.

"His boss said, 'What are you doing? You should be on guard!' He said to his boss, 'But my children are sick. They might die! I have to go!' Luckily, the officer was his friend. He said, 'OK, you go. I understand. I hope your children are OK. I won't tell anyone.' George said, 'Thank you Sir. Thank you so much.' And he hurried back to Springhill House."

Peter and I stood outside the entrance to the house. I imagined George running through the doors.

"And what happened? Were his children OK?" I asked.

"Well, when he arrived home, his wife, Olivia, was waiting for him. She said, 'The children are not in danger anymore! They are getting better!' George was so relieved. He ran into his children's bedroom and looked at his children. They smiled when they saw their father."

"That's a happy ending," I said.

"Oh wait, Old Jack. I haven't finished," said Peter. We started walking again, along a small path through the garden.

"When George returned to the army, he got a very bad shock. His friend, the officer, had told the commander. George had trusted his friend, but his friend betrayed him! So George was in a lot of trouble. He was also very ashamed. He had to leave the army. He lost his job. When he returned home, he was very sad and depressed. Then, soon after, his daughter died. He became even more depressed."

"That's terrible," I said.

"Yes, but the story gets worse," said Peter. "George was sad and depressed for two years. Then, one night, he took his gun into a room called the Blue Room.

"His wife, Olivia, heard him go into the room. She was very worried. She ran to the room, but she was too late. When she arrived at the room, George shot himself."

"That's terrible! So his ghost lives in Springhill House?" I asked.

"No, it isn't the ghost of George. It is the ghost of Olivia."

"Olivia?"

"Yes. Many years ago, a woman was staying at Springhill House. When she walked past the Blue Room, she was very shocked. She saw a woman. The woman looked very upset. Her hands were in the air, and she looked like she was screaming. Then, the woman disappeared. Another woman was staying in the Blue Room, and she felt something strange. She felt people running around, and panicking. But there was no one there."

"Has Olivia only been seen once?" I asked.

"No, she has been seen many times. People often see her ghost running to the Blue Room. She runs to the room to save George. But she is too late. One time, when the family was still living at the house, they saw the ghost of Olivia looking at the children in their beds. She was smiling. She is a friendly ghost."

I turned around and looked at the house. It was a beautiful house, even under the grey winter sky.

"This is a peaceful place," I said. "I hope Olivia can find peace here, one day."

5. THE BEAST

Place: Leap Castle, County Offaly

We travelled south, back into the Republic of Ireland. We were lucky. It was a beautiful sunny day. It was cold, but the sky was blue.

"Do you want to see one of the most frightening castles in Ireland?" asked Peter.

"Yes, of course," I said. "Where is it?"

"It's Leap Castle, in County Offaly. We can't go inside, because we don't have a reservation, but we can see it from the outside."

"How many ghosts are there?" I asked.

"I don't know. Let's stop for a rest in a pub in the local town of Roscrea. Maybe one of the local people can tell us."

We arrived in the town late in the afternoon. We found a pub and sat at the bar. I had some whiskey, as usual, and Peter had some orange juice.

A man was sitting next to us. He heard me speaking, and said, "Are you from England?"

"Yes," I said. "I'm travelling around Ireland, looking for ghosts."

The man laughed. Then, he stopped laughing. He looked at me and said,

"Do you know about Leap Castle?"

"Yes," said Peter. "But could you tell us about the ghosts?"

"Sure," said the man.

This is the story he told us.

Leap Castle was built in the 13th century. It has a long and sad history. The owners were a strong and violent family, called the

14

O'Carrolls. In the 16th century, the head of the O'Carroll family died. The other family members started fighting. They all wanted to be the new leader. In particular, there were two brothers who wanted to become the head of the family. One of the brothers was a priest.

A hall in the castle was used as a chapel, or small church. One day, the brother who was a priest was performing a mass for the family in the chapel. He had just started to pray, when his brother came into the chapel. His brother was very angry. He said, "You started saying prayers without me! Why didn't you wait for me?"

He was so angry, that he killed his brother, the priest, in the chapel, in front of the other family members. Since then, the ghost of the priest has been seen in the chapel. But this is not the most frightening ghost of the castle. There is a room next to the chapel. This room is called the 'oubliette'. This is a French word. It comes from the French word for 'to forget'.

When the O'Carrolls caught an enemy, or had a fight with someone, they threw the person into this room. They "forgot" about the person, so the person died a very slow death, with no food or water. The O'Carrolls killed many people this way.

In the early 20th century, another family was living in the castle. They decided to repair and clean the castle. One day, workmen went into the oubliette. They found many bones and skeletons. These were the bones and skeletons of the people who had been thrown into the room. The workmen took out the bones and skeletons, and after that, very strange things happened.

The lady of the castle, Mildred Darby, was interested in ghosts and spirits. She often tried to communicate with ghosts. One day, she had a very bad experience. First, there was a terrible smell. It was the smell of a dead body. Then, a ghost appeared. It was an evil ghost, called an 'elemental'. It was half-human, half-beast, with big black holes in the place of eyes.

People say that elementals appear in places with lots of bad or sad energy. They say that when the workmen found the skeletons in the oubliette, the elemental spirit woke up. So, when Lady Darby tried to contact a ghost, she contacted the elemental.

Then, in 1922, there was a big fire at the castle. After that, no one lived in it for a long time. For many years after the fire, local people saw bright candle lights in the chapel window. The local people were very frightened, so they would not go near the castle at night.

The castle became very famous for its ghosts. Now, the castle is owned by another family. Over the years, many spiritual people have visited the castle. They have told the evil spirits to go away. But the ghosts haven't gone away. The ghosts are still there, but they are not evil any more. Some local people still see the candle light in the chapel window on dark nights, and some people have seen the ghost of the priest in the chapel.

When the man finished telling us the story, Peter said to me, "Shall we take a look? We can't go inside because we have no reservation, but maybe we can see the outside."

"OK," I said. "But if we go in daylight we won't see the candlelight. Let's wait until it gets dark."

"OK," said Peter. "Let's have another drink first."

6. THE DEVIL'S FOOT

Place: Loftus Hall, Hook Head, County Wexford

It was a sunny morning. Peter and I were driving south, to County Wexford.

I said to Peter, "The story the man told us in the bar in Roscrea about Leap Castle was interesting. Half-human half-beast ghosts are unusual."

Peter smiled. "Not so unusual," he said. "I'm taking you to Wexford because there is another half-human half-beast ghost."

"Another one?" I asked.

"Yes, and I think this one is more frightening."

After a long drive, we stopped at a restaurant called the Templars Inn for lunch.

"So," I said to Peter. "Tell me about the ghost."

"Well, there is a very large house called Loftus Hall. It is here on Hook Peninsula, next to the sea. It was built in the fourteenth century. In the eighteenth century, a man called Charles Tottenham lived there with his wife and daughter. His daughter's name was Anne. One night, there was a terrible storm. The family was in the living room, when they heard a knock at the door.

"When Charles opened the door, he saw a handsome young man. 'Please,' said the man. 'There is a storm. My ship is damaged. I need a place to stay. May I stay here until the storm passes?' 'Of course,' said Charles. 'Come in.'

"The family welcomed the young man. Anne thought the man was very handsome. She became very close to the stranger with the beautiful smile. The family liked the man too, and they let him stay for a few days.

"One night, the family and the man were in the living room. They were playing a card game. Anne looked at everyone. *Everyone has five cards. I only have four cards. Why?* she thought. Then, she saw a card on the floor. She bent down under the table to pick the card up. Then, she saw the man's feet. They were not human feet. They were horse's feet! He had feet like a horse!"

I stopped eating and looked at Peter. "No!" I said. "I don't believe it!"

"Oh yes. This is true," said Peter. "Anne started to scream. Then suddenly, the young man flew up to the ceiling, and went through the roof! There was a very large hole in the roof, and they never saw the man again. After that, Anne became mentally ill. She stayed in a room, sitting in a chair, looking out at the sea, waiting for the young man to come back. After some years, she died, still sitting in the chair."

"What happened after that?" I asked.

"Well, the family tried to repair the hole in the roof, but they couldn't. Maybe the evil spirit of the man stopped them. And after that, strange things started to happen in the house. So, the family asked the local churchman to come to the house. They asked him to pray and tell the spirit to go away. The churchman came, but it had no effect. The spirit of the man stayed in the house. Next, they asked a Catholic priest to come to the house. The priest's name was Father Thomas Broaders. He told the spirit to go away. After that, the spirit became quiet, but it didn't go away.

"Then, in the nineteenth century, the house was re-built."

"When they built the new house, did the spirit go away?" I asked.

"No, it didn't," said Peter. "In the new house, staff saw the ghost of a young girl. They think it was Anne. And they heard the sound of running horses…"

I didn't say anything for a while. I tried to imagine that night, when Anne saw the man's strange feet.

Then, I asked, "Do people live in Loftus Hall today?"

"No," said Peter. "It's empty now. But there are ghost tours of the house. Would you like to go on the tour?"

"I'd like that very much," I said.

"Well, let's reserve a night time tour," said Peter. "I think the night time tour will be more interesting. We might see a ghost."

I smiled. "OK," I said. "I'm old now, but I'm not too old for an adventure!"

THANK YOU

Thank you for reading Old Jack's Ghost Stories from Ireland. (Word count: 5,046) Old Jack hopes you enjoyed reading his stories.

For more information about the places in this book, please visit http://www.italk-youtalk.com. There is a page with maps and photographs of the places that Old Jack has written about.

If you would like to read more graded readers, please visit our website http://www.italkyoutalk.com

Other graded readers by Old Jack:
Old Jack's Ghost Stories from England (1)
Old Jack's Ghost Stories from England (2)
Old Jack's Ghost Stories from Scotland
Old Jack's Ghost Stories from Wales
Old Jack's Ghost Stories from Japan

NOTES AND REFERENCES

1. Cromwell's Friend
Malahide Castle & Gardens, Malahide, County Dublin
The story is based on information found on the following sites:
http://www.malahidecastleandgardens.ie/TheCastle/HistoryOvervie
w/
(Retrieved May 2014)
http://en.wikipedia.org/wiki/Malahide_Castle (Retrieved May 2014)
http://www.hauntedrooms.co.uk/malahide-castle-dublin-ireland
(Retrieved May 2014)
http://www.mysteriousbritain.co.uk/republic-of-
ireland/dublin/hauntings/malahide-castle.html (Retrieved May 2014)

2. Coming Home
Castle Leslie Estate, Glaslough, County Monaghan
The story is based on information found on the following site:
http://www.castleleslie.com/castle-hotels-ireland.html#
(Retrieved May 2014)

3. Knock Knock
Ballygally Castle Hotel, 274 Coast Road, Ballygally, County Antrim,
BT40 2QZ
The story is based on information found on the following site and in
the following book:
http://en.wikipedia.org/wiki/Ballygally_Castle
(Retrieved May 2014)

Belanger, Jeff. World's Most Haunted Places (New York: The Rosen Publishing Group, 2009) Pages 15-20

4. The Betrayal
20 Springhill Road, Moneymore, Magherafelt, County Londonderry, BT45 7NQ
The story is based on information found on the following sites:
http://www.nationaltrust.org.uk/springhill/ (Retrieved May 2014)
http://en.wikipedia.org/wiki/Springhill_House (Retrieved May 2014)
http://www.haunted-britain.com/Haunted_Irleland_North.htm (Retrieved May 2014)

5. The Beast
Leap Castle, Roscrea, County Offaly, Ireland
The story is based on information found on the following sites and in the following book:
http://en.wikipedia.org/wiki/Leap_Castle (Retrieved May 2014)
http://leapcastle.net/ (Retrieved May 2014)
Vale, Allison. Hell House: And Other True Hauntings from Around the World. (New York: Gusto Company AS, Sterling Publishing Co., Inc., 2005) Pages 112-115

6. The Devil's Foot
Loftus Hall, Hook Head, New Ross, County Wexford
The story is based on information found on the following sites:
http://en.wikipedia.org/wiki/Loftus_Hall (Retrieved May 2014)
http://www.abandonedireland.com/Loftus_Hall_2.html (Retrieved May 2014)

ABOUT THE AUTHOR

I Talk You Talk Press is a Japan-based publisher of language textbooks, graded readers and language learning/teaching resources.

Our team is made up of highly experienced language teachers and translators, who have all studied at least one additional language to an advanced level.

This experience enables us to design our materials from the perspective of both the teacher and the learner. We consult with both teachers and language learners when designing our textbooks and graded readers, and test our materials extensively in the classroom before publication.

We are a fast-growing press, and currently publish graded readers for learners of English. We publish new graded readers monthly.

www.ingramcontent.com/pod-product-compliance
Lightning Source LLC
Chambersburg PA
CBHW022352040426
42449CB00006B/838